NEW ENGLAND SEAFOOD COOKING

Designed by Claire Leighton
Recipe photography by Peter Barry and Jean-Paul Paireault
Recipes styled by Bridgeen Deery and Wendy Devenish
Edited by Jillian Stewart

CLB 2987
© 1993 Colour Library Books Ltd, Godalming, Surrey, England.
All rights reserved.
This 1993 edition published by Crescent Books,
distributed by Outlet Book Company Inc., a Random House Company,
40 Engelhard Avenue, Avenel, New Jersey 07001.
Printed and bound in Singapore.
ISBN 0 517 07300 5
8 7 6 5 4 3 2 1

NEW ENGLAND SEAFOOD COOKING

CRESCENT BOOKS
NEW YORK · AVENEL, NEW JERSEY

INTRODUCTION

New England is renowned the world over for its fine seafood, and no trip to the area is complete without a taste of one of these seafood delights. The secret of the region's delicious seafood cuisine lies in the use of the finest, freshest fish, and the enhancement of the often delicate flavors with the simplest of sauces and accompaniments. What better way to enjoy Maine lobster, for example, than to simply boil it and then serve it with butter?

This tasty, yet essentially plain, way of cooking has its origins with New England's early pioneer settlers. These Puritan settlers, religious dissidents seeking to break from the ceremonial display that characterized the established churches in Europe, came to make a new life for themselves in America. Their lives were both simple and frugal, not only because this is what the harsh conditions of New England in the seventeenth century demanded, but because it was an important part of their belief. They utilized the natural resources of the area, of which fish and seafood were among the most plentiful. Cod, scrod, lobster, crab, and clams were, and still are, found in abundance in the cold Atlantic waters off the coast of New England.

Though the influence of these early New Englanders on the region's cuisine may be the most enduring, other factors have also played an important part in its development. The Puritans were not the only ones to come to America in search of a new life. Waves of immigration in the nineteenth century brought Italians and Irish to big cities like Boston, and with these immigrants came innovations in the style of cooking with the introduction of new ingredients.

Today, as the health risks posed by a diet high in red meat become more publicized, many more people eat fish on a regular basis. Seafood is deservedly a popular alternative to meat and poultry, for like them it is a complete protein, and is high in vitamins and minerals. Unlike red meat, however, fish is relatively low in fat. Indeed medical evidence suggests that oily fish, such as mackerel, may even help to reduce high blood cholesterol levels. In addition to its nutritional benefits, fish is quick and easy to cook and very versatile.

This collection of New England seafood recipes enables you to recreate the flavors of one of America's finest cooking traditions. The recipes introduce some of the main techniques for preparing and cooking fish and shellfish, and provide innovative ideas for serving and presenting this invaluable source of protein.

Right: the day's catch being sorted at Newport, Rhode Island. The town is one of New England's busiest ports.

Clam Chowder

Preparation Time: 30 minutes **Cooking Time:** 20 minutes **Serves:** 6-8

This legendary New England dish uses the delicious varieties of clams found along the coastline.

Ingredients

2 lbs clams
3 oz bacon, diced
2 medium onions, finely diced
1 tbsp flour
6 medium potatoes, peeled and cubed

Salt and pepper
4 cups milk
1 cup light cream
Chopped parsley

Scrub the clams well and place in a sink (or bowl) of cold water with a handful of flour for 30 minutes. Drain the clams and place them in a deep saucepan with about ½ cup cold water. Cover and bring to a boil, stirring occasionally until all the shells open. Discard any shells that do not open. Strain the clam liquid, reserve it, and set the clams aside to cool.

Place the bacon in a large, deep saucepan and cook slowly until the fat is rendered. Turn up the heat and brown the bacon. Remove it to paper towels to drain. Add the onion to the bacon fat in the pan and cook slowly to soften. Stir in the flour and add the potatoes, salt, pepper, milk and reserved clam juice. Cover and bring to a boil and cook for about 10 minutes, or until the potatoes are nearly tender. Remove the clams from their shells and chop them if large. Add to the soup along with the cream and diced bacon. Cook 10 minutes more, or until the potatoes and clams are tender. Add the chopped parsley and serve immediately.

Top: sunset over Princetown, Massachusetts.

Mussel Soup

Preparation Time: 15 minutes **Cooking Time:** 20 minutes **Serves:** 4

Crusty white bread is the perfect accompaniment for this soup.

Ingredients

2 quarts fresh mussels
¼ cup butter
2 onions, peeled and finely chopped
2 cloves garlic, crushed
1¼ cups dry white wine

1¼ cups water
2 tbsps lemon juice
2 oz fresh bread crumbs
2 tbsps freshly chopped parsley
Salt and freshly ground black pepper

Scrub the mussels with a stiff brush and remove any barnacle shells or pieces of seaweed that are attached to them. Tap each mussel sharply and discard any that do not close tightly. Melt the butter in large saucepan and gently fry the onions and garlic until soft, but not browned. Add the mussels, wine, water and lemon juice to the pan, and bring to a boil. Season with salt and pepper, then cover and cook for approximately 10 minutes or until all the mussel shells have completely opened. Discard any mussels that have not opened fully. Strain the mussels through a colander and return the juices and stock to the saucepan. Put the mussels in a serving tureen and keep warm. Add the bread crumbs and the parsley to the mussel juices and bring them to a boil. Adjust the seasoning, and serve over the mussels in the tureen. Serve immediately.

Bass Harbor Light on Mount Desert Island. The island is a popular summer retreat.

New England Bouillabaisse

Preparation Time: 35 minutes **Cooking Time:** 30 minutes **Serves:** 4

French settlers brought this favorite recipe to the New World, and just as they would have at home, they used local, seasonal ingredients in it.

Ingredients

Stock
1 lb fish bones, skin and heads
7 cups water
1 small onion, thinly sliced
1 small carrot, thinly sliced
1 bay leaf
6 black peppercorns
¼ tsp powdered mace
1 sprig fresh thyme or ½ tsp dried
2 lemon slices

Bouillabaisse
⅓ cup butter or margarine
1 carrot, sliced

3 leeks, well washed and thinly sliced
1 clove garlic
Pinch saffron
⅓-½ cup dry white wine
8 oz canned tomatoes
1 lobster
1 lb cod fillets
1 lb mussels, well scrubbed
1 lb small clams, well scrubbed
8 new potatoes, scrubbed but
  not peeled
Chopped parsley
8 oz large shrimp, peeled and de-veined

Place all the stock ingredients in a large stock pot and bring to a boil over high heat. Lower the heat and allow to simmer for 20 minutes. Strain and reserve the stock, discarding the fish bones and vegetables. Melt the butter in a medium-sized saucepan and add the carrot, leeks and garlic. Cook for about 5 minutes until slightly softened. Add the saffron and wine and simmer for 5 minutes. Add the fish stock along with the remaining bouillabaisse ingredients except the shrimp. Bring the mixture to a boil and cook until the lobster turns red, the mussel and clam shells open and the potatoes are tender. Turn off the heat and add the shrimp. Cover the pan and let the shrimp cook in the residual heat. Divide the ingredients into soup bowls. Remove the lobster, cut in half lengthwise and remove the sand sac. Divide the tail between 2 serving bowls and serve the bouillabaisse with garlic bread.

Salmon Pâté

Preparation Time: 15 minutes   **Serves:** 4

This highly nutritious, elegant pâté is low in fat and very quick to prepare.

Ingredients

8 oz fresh or canned red or pink
   salmon, drained
½ cup low fat cottage cheese
Few drops lemon juice
Pinch ground mace or
   ground nutmeg

¼ tsp Tabasco sauce
Freshly ground sea salt and
   black pepper
2 tbsps low-fat natural yogurt
4 small pickles

Remove any bones and skin from the salmon. Mix the fish to a smooth paste in a food processor. Beat the cottage cheese until it is smooth. Add the salmon, lemon juice, seasonings, and natural yogurt to the cottage cheese and mix well until thoroughly incorporated. Divide the mixture equally among 4 individual custard cups. Smooth the surfaces carefully. Slice each pickle lengthways 4 or 5 times, making sure that you do not cut right through the pickle at the narrow end. Splay the cut ends into a fan and use these to decorate the tops of the pâtés.

Quincy Market in Boston is a colorful, busy area filled with restaurants and stalls.

Oysters à la Crème

Preparation Time: 15 minutes **Cooking Time:** about 5 minutres **Serves:** 4

Oysters can be bought out of season but they are expensive, so try this recipe when you can buy them fresh from the fish market.

Ingredients
2 dozen oysters on the half shell
   or unopened
4 tbsps heavy cream
4 tbsps cream cheese

1 tbsp chopped fresh parsley
Salt and pepper
Nutmeg
Cilantro leaves to garnish

Scrub the oyster shells well, if unopened, and leave to soak in clean water for 2 hours. Insert a short-bladed knife near the hinge and pry open. Remove any pieces of broken shell from the inside and press the oysters in a circle onto a baking pan filled with rock salt. Mix together the heavy cream, cream cheese, parsley and salt and pepper. Top each oyster with the cream mixture. Sprinkle with nutmeg and place in a preheated oven at 350°F for 18-20 minutes. Garnish with cilantro leaves and serve immediately.

The *Beaver II* in Boston harbor, a replica of one of the original "Tea Party" ships.

Cape Cod Mussels

Preparation Time: 30 minutes **Cooking Time:** 5-8 minutes **Serves:** 4

When seafood is as good as that from Cape Cod, even the simplest prepararations stand out.

Ingredients

4½ lbs mussels in their shells
Flour or cornmeal
1 cup dry white wine
1 large onion, finely chopped
2-4 cloves garlic, finely chopped

Salt and coarsely ground black pepper
2 bay leaves
1 cup butter, melted
Juice of 1 lemon

Scrub the mussels well and remove any barnacles and beards. Use a stiff brush to scrub the shells, and discard any mussels with broken shells or those that do not close when tapped. Place the mussels in a sink (or bowl) full of cold water with a handful of flour or cornmeal and leave to soak for 30 minutes. Drain the mussels and place them in a large, deep saucepan with the remaining ingredients, except the butter and lemon juice. Cover the pan and bring to a boil. Stir the mussels occasionally while they are cooking to help them cook evenly. Cook about 5-8 minutes, or until the shells open. Discard any mussels that do not open. Spoon the mussels into individual serving bowls and strain the cooking liquid. Pour the liquid into 4 small bowls and serve with the mussels and a bowl of melted butter mixed with lemon juice for each person. Dip the mussels into the broth and the melted butter to eat. Use a mussel shell to scoop out each mussel, or eat with small forks.

Cape Cod's graceful curve ends at Wood End and Long Point.

Scallops in Saffron Sauce

Preparation Time: 15 minutes **Cooking Time:** about 15 minutes **Serves:** 4

Scallops are in season during fall and winter so prepare this unusual dish when they are at their freshest.

Ingredients

16 large scallops
½ cup water
½ cup dry white wine
1 shallot, roughly chopped
1 bouquet garni, consisting of
   1 bay leaf, 1 sprig of fresh thyme
   and 3 stalks of parsley

6 black peppercorns
A few strands of saffron
4 tbsps hot water
1¼ cups heavy cream
3 tbsps fresh chopped parsley
Salt and pepper

Put the scallops into a large shallow pan together with the water, wine, shallot, bouquet garnis and peppercorns. Cover the pan and bring the liquid almost to a boil. Remove the pan from the heat and leave the scallops to poach in the hot liquid for 10-15 minutes. The scallops are cooked when they are just firm to the touch. Remove them from the liquid and keep warm on a plate. Strain the scallop cooking liquid into a small saucepan and bring to a boil. Allow the liquid to boil rapidly until it is reduced by about half. Soak the saffron in the hot water for about 5 minutes, or until the color has infused into the water. Add the saffron with its soaking liquid, the heavy cream and the chopped parsley to the reduced cooking liquid and season to taste. Bring the sauce to just below boiling point. Arrange the scallops on a serving plate and pour some of the sauce over them before serving. Serve the remaining sauce separately.

The New England coastline is dotted with restaurants serving fresh seafood.

Swordfish Kebabs

Preparation Time: 15 minutes **Cooking Time:** about 10 minutes **Serves:** 4-6

Swordfish is perfect for kebabs as it is firm-fleshed and holds its shape well when cut.

Ingredients

2¼ lbs swordfish steaks	1 lb cherry tomatoes
6 tbsps olive oil	2 lemons, cut in thin slices
1 tsp dried oregano	Salt and freshly ground pepper
1 tsp dried marjoram	Lemon slices and cilantro leaves
Juice and rind of ½ a lemon	for garnish

Cut the swordfish steaks into 2-inch pieces. Mix the olive oil, herbs, lemon juice and rind together and set aside. Thread the swordfish, tomato slices and lemon slices on skewers, alternating the ingredients. Brush the skewers with the oil and lemon juice mixture and cook under a preheated broiler for about 10 minutes, basting frequently. Serve garnished with lemons and cilantro.

Top: Edgartown, on Martha's Vineyard – once a famous whaling port.

Fried Squid

Preparation Time: 25 minutes   **Cooking Time:** 3 minutes per batch of 6
Serves: 4

Squid was once caught off the New England coast and taken to Mediterranean countries where it is a great favorite. Nowadays it's a popular food here, too.

Ingredients

1½ lbs squid, cleaned and cut into
   rings
½ cup all-purpose flour
Salt and pepper

Oil for deep-frying
Lemon wedges and parsley
   for garnishing

Mix the flour, salt and pepper together on a sheet of paper or in a shallow dish. Toss the rings of squid in the flour mixture to coat. Heat the oil to 350°F and fry the squid, about 6 pieces at a time.

   Remove them from the oil when brown and crisp and place on paper towels. Sprinkle lightly with salt and continue with the remaining squid. The pieces will take about 3 minutes to cook. Place on serving dishes and garnish each dish with a wedge of lemon and some parsley.

The sun sets over New England's rugged coastline.

Mussels in Red Wine

Preparation Time: 30 minutes **Cooking Time:** 10 minutes **Serves:** 4

Mussels are low in calories and an excellent source of potassium. They are now becoming more popular as people realize their nutritional value.

Ingredients

3 lbs mussels, well scrubbed
1 cup dry red wine
6 tbsps olive oil
4 cloves garlic, finely chopped
2 bay leaves
1 tbsp dried thyme
6 tbsps red wine vinegar

1 tsp paprika
Grated juice and rind of 1 lemon
Salt and pepper
Pinch cayenne pepper
Pinch sugar
Chopped parsley

Scrub the mussels well to remove beards and barnacles. Discard any with broken shells or those that do not close when tapped. Leave the mussels to soak in water with a handful of flour for 30 minutes.

Place the wine in a large saucepan and bring to a boil. Add the mussels, cover the pan and cook briskly for about 4-5 minutes, stirring frequently, until the shells open. Discard any that do not open. Transfer the mussels to a bowl and pour the cooking liquid through a fine strainer and reserve it. In a clean saucepan, heat the oil and fry the garlic over gentle heat until golden brown. Add the bay leaves, thyme, vinegar, paprika, lemon juice and rind, salt, pepper and cayenne pepper. Pour in the wine, add sugar and bring to a boil. Cook to reduce to about ⅔ cup. Allow to cool completely. Remove the mussels from their shells and add them to the liquid, stirring to coat all the mussels. Cover and place in the refrigerator for at least 2 hours. Allow to stand at room temperature for 30 minutes before serving. Sprinkle with parsley.

Two Lights State Park, near Portland, Maine.

Monkfish Kebabs with Butter Sauce

Preparation Time: 30 minutes **Cooking Time:** 25 minutes **Serves:** 4

Monkfish is a good choice for kebabs as its flesh is white, firm-textured, and has a good flavor.

Ingredients

8 strips bacon
1 tsp grated lemon rind
2 lbs monkfish, cut into
   2-inch pieces
1 green pepper, seeded and cut
   into 2-inch pieces
1 red pepper, seeded and cut into
   2-inch pieces
12 button mushrooms, washed
   and trimmed

8 bay leaves
Oil for brushing
½ cup dry white wine
4 tbsps tarragon vinegar
2 shallots, finely chopped
1 tsp dried tarragon
1 tbsp chopped fresh chervil or parsley
1 cup butter, melted
Salt and pepper

Cut the bacon in half lengthwise and then in half across. Place a piece of fish on each strip of bacon and sprinkle with the lemon rind. Roll up the bacon around the fish. Thread each fish and bacon roll onto kebab skewers, alternating with the peppers, mushrooms and bay leaves. Brush well with oil. Cook under a broiler for 15 minutes, turning frequently and brushing with more oil, if necessary, until the fish is cooked. Heat the wine, vinegar and shallots together in a small saucepan until boiling. Cook rapidly until reduced by half. Stir in the herbs and lower the heat. Beat in the butter, a little at a time, until the sauce is thick. Season to taste and serve with the kebabs.

Shrimp Salad

Preparation Time: 25-30 minutes plus 2 hours refrigeration **Serves:** 4-6

Shrimp freezes so well it can be used all year round.

Ingredients
2 lbs peeled uncooked shrimp

Marinade
1 cup sweet white wine
4 tbsps lemon juice
1 tbsp chopped fresh dill
Pinch salt and black pepper

1 clove garlic, crushed
1 bay leaf
4 tbsps butter or margarine

Lettuce
Chopped parsley for garnishing

Peel the shrimp and remove the black vein along the top if desired. Place the shrimp in a shallow dish. Combine all the marinade ingredients except the butter. Pour the marinade over the shrimp and and turn several times to coat well. Marinate for at least 2 hours in the refrigerator.

Melt the butter or margarine in a large frying pan. Remove the shrimp from the marinade with a slotted spoon and place them in the butter. Cook over moderate heat for 8-10 minutes, stirring frequently. Pour the marinade into a deep saucepan. Boil rapidly until it thickens and reduces by about ¾. Place the cooked shrimp in a shallow dish, pour on the reduced marinade and chill well. To serve, line a large serving dish or individual dishes with lettuce, place the shrimp and reduced marinade on top and sprinkle with chopped parsley.

Sunset over Boston highlights Beacon Hill, an area famous for its elegant architecture and its gas-lit, tree-lined streets.

Eel in Red Wine

Preparation Time: 20 minutes **Cooking Time:** 25 minutes **Serves:** 4

Eel are plentiful in Cape waters and can be bought ready-cleaned from the fish market if you don't want to do it yourself.

Ingredients

1¼ lbs eel, skinned
Salt and pepper
2 tbsps olive oil
2 onions, finely sliced
1 clove garlic, chopped

1¼ cups red wine
1 tsp sugar
3 tbsp tomato paste
½ cup fish stock

Cut the eel into medium-thick slices and season with salt and pepper. Heat the oil and fry the onion and garlic for 1 minute. Add the eel slices to the pan and sear on both sides. Stir the wine and sugar into the pan, cook until the wine reduces, then add the tomato paste and the fish stock. Season with salt and pepper if necessary. Transfer to an ovenproof dish and finish cooking in a medium oven for 15 minutes. Remove the eel from the dish and if the sauce is not very thick, pour it into a saucepan and thicken and reduce it over high heat. Serve hot, with the sauce poured over.

Top: a colorful selection of buoys brightens a fishing shed in New Hampshire.

Salt Cod with Peppers

Preparation Time: 50 minutes plus 24 hours soaking
Cooking Time: 1 hour 20 minutes   **Serves:** 6

Salt cod is combined with peppers, chili and garlic in this new treatment of a New England favorite.

Ingredients

2 lbs salt cod	3 tbsps olive oil
2 red peppers	4 tbsps heavy cream
2 green peppers	2 tbsps chopped parsley
3 large onions	2 tomatoes, peeled, seeded
6 cloves garlic	and chopped
1 small red chili pepper	Salt and pepper
5 large potatoes	Fresh chervil to garnish

Cut the salt cod into pieces. Soak in water for 24 hours, changing the water several times. Cut the peppers, remove the seeds and white pith and slice into strips. Peel and chop the onions finely. Chop the garlic. Seed and chop the chili pepper. Peel the potatoes, quarter them and cook in boiling salted water for 30 minutes with 1 chopped onion and 1 tbsp of olive oil. Drain the potatoes and onions when cooled. Blend until smooth or press through a sieve. Add the cream and parsley, and season to taste. Bring the soaked and drained cod to a boil in a large quantity of water and cook for 5 minutes. Set aside to drain and cool. Flake with your fingers, discarding the skin and bones. Fry the chopped garlic and chili pepper in 3½ tbsps oil until soft and lightly colored. Add the peppers and the two remaining onions. Cook for 10 minutes over a moderate heat, stirring well. Add the tomatoes to the peppers and onions, and cook for another 15 minutes, stirring frequently. Season to taste.

Oil the bottom of an ovenproof pan or individual pie dishes. Arrange a layer of the potato purée over the bottom. Spread the cod over it. Top with a layer of the pepper, onion and tomato mixture. Bake in a hot oven at 400°F for 30 minutes. Serve hot garnished with chopped chervil.

Swordfish Steaks with Peppercorn and Garlic Sauce

Preparation Time: 25 minutes plus overnight soaking
Cooking Time: 15 minutes   **Serves:** 4

This unusual sauce perfectly enhances the delicious swordfish found off New England's coastline during the summer months.

Ingredients

2 tbsps fresh green peppercorns	1 egg
6 tbsps lemon juice	1 clove garlic, roughly chopped
4 tbsps olive oil	⅓ cup oil
Freshly ground sea salt	1 tsp dried oregano
4 swordfish steaks	Salt and freshly ground black pepper

Crush the green peppercorns lightly using a mortar and pestle. Mix the lemon juice, olive oil and salt into the lightly crushed green peppercorns. Place the swordfish steaks in a shallow ovenproof dish and pour the lemon and oil mixture over each steak. Refrigerate overnight, turning once or twice.

Using a blender or food processor, mix together the egg and garlic. With the machine still running, gradually pour the oil through the funnel in a thin steady stream onto the egg and garlic mixture. Continue to blend until the sauce is thick. Preheat the broiler and arrange the swordfish on the broiler rack. Sprinkle the oregano over the swordfish steaks and season well. Cook for 15 minutes, turning them frequently and basting with the lemon and pepper marinade. When the steaks are cooked place onto a serving dish and spoon the garlic mayonnaise over them to serve.

Lobster Salad

Preparation Time: 25 minutes   **Serves:** 3-4

No book on seafood would be complete without a lobster salad and this one is extra special with the addition of cooked chicken.

Ingredients

Salad
1 large cooked lobster
2 cooked chicken breasts
4 sticks celery
3 oz browned cashew nuts
4 green onions
1 head Chinese cabbage
1 head curly endive
4 oz snow peas

Dressing
1¼ cups mayonnaise
2 tbsps soy sauce
1 tsp honey
Sesame seed oil
½ tsp ground ginger
1 tbsp dry sherry (optional)

Garnish
1 red pepper, thinly sliced
2 tbsps chopped parsley

Twist off the claws and legs of the lobster. Cut the body in half, take out the tail meat and set aside. Crack claws and remove meat. Remove as much meat as possible from all the legs. Cut chicken breast meat into thin, even slices. Reserve the meat from 1 breast and mix the remaining shredded chicken with the meat from the lobster claws and legs. Cut lobster tail meat lengthwise into 3-4 thin slices. Set lobster tail meat aside with the reserved chicken meat. Mix celery, cashew nuts and green onions together with the shredded lobster and chicken. Mix the dressing ingredients together, adding ground black pepper and salt if necessary. Mix the dressing with the shredded lobster and chicken. Slice red pepper into thin strips. Slice Chinese cabbage into thin strips. Tear curly endive leaves into pieces. Pile the greens and snow peas onto a large serving dish. Mound the shredded lobster and chicken salad in the middle. Arrange some sliced chicken breast and the lobster tail neatly over the top. Garnish with sliced red pepper and chopped parsley. Serve any remaining dressing separately.

Boston Scrod

Preparation Time: 15 minutes **Cooking Time:** 12 minutes **Serves:** 4

Scrod, or baby codfish, provides the perfect base for a crunchy, slightly spicy topping. Boston is justly famous for it.

Ingredients

4 even-sized cod fillets
Salt and pepper
⅓ cup butter, melted
¾ cup dry breadcrumbs
1 tsp dry mustard

1 tsp onion salt
Dash Worcester sauce and Tabasco
2 tbsps lemon juice
1 tbsp finely chopped parsley

Season the fish fillets with salt and pepper and place them on a broiler tray. Brush with butter and broil for about 5 minutes. Combine remaining butter with breadcrumbs, mustard, onion salt, Worcester sauce, Tabasco, lemon juice and parsley. Spoon the mixture carefully on top of each fish fillet, covering it completely. Press down lightly to pack the crumbs into place. Broil for another 5-7 minutes, or until the top is lightly browned and the fish flakes.

A quiet stretch of shoreline at Cape Cod, Massachusetts.

Whole Baked Fish with New England Stuffing

Preparation Time: 25 minutes **Cooking Time:** 40 minutes **Serves:** 4

A whole fish, perfectly cooked, never fails to impress. With a stuffing of oysters, it is certainly grand enough for an important dinner party.

Ingredients

4½ lbs whole fish, cleaned and
   boned (use salmon, salmon trout
   or sea bass)

Stuffing
8 oz savory bread crumbs
¼ cup butter, melted

Pinch salt and pepper
2 tsps lemon juice
¼ tsp each dried thyme, sage
   and marjoram
1 shallot, finely chopped
10 oysters, shelled

Buy the fish cleaned and boned, but with the head and tail still on. Rinse the fish inside and out and pat dry. Place the fish on lightly oiled foil. Combine all the stuffing ingredients, mixing carefully so that the oysters do not fall apart. Open the cavity of the fish and spoon in the stuffing. Close the fish and pat gently so that the stuffing is evenly distributed. Close the foil loosely around the fish and place it directly on the oven shelf or in a large roasting pan. Cook at 400°F for about 40 minutes. Unwrap the fish and slide it onto a serving plate. Peel off the top layer of skin if desired and garnish with lemon slices.

New Hampshire has over 1,300 lakes and ponds, offering ample fishing.

Boatman's Stew

Preparation Time: 20 minutes **Cooking Time:** 45 minutes **Serves:** 4-6

This quick, economical and satisfying fish dish will please any fish lover for lunch or a light supper.

Ingredients

6 tbsps olive oil
2 large onions, sliced
1 red pepper, seeded and sliced
4 oz mushrooms, sliced
1 lb canned tomatoes
Pinch salt and pepper

Pinch dried thyme
1½ cups water
2 lbs whitefish fillets, skinned
½ cup white wine
2 tbsps chopped parsley
French bread

Heat the oil in a large saucepan and add the onions. Cook until beginning to look translucent. Add the red pepper and cook until the vegetables are softened. Add the mushrooms and tomatoes and bring the mixture to a boil. Add thyme, salt, pepper and water and simmer for about 30 minutes. Add the fish and wine and cook until the fish flakes easily – about 15 minutes. Stir in the parsley.

To serve, place a piece of toasted French bread in the bottom of the soup bowl and spoon the fish stew over it.

Top: the picturesque fishing village of Menemsha, on Martha's Vineyard.

Boiled Maine Lobster

Preparation Time: 20 minutes **Cooking Time:** 15 minutes **Serves:** 4

With today's lobster prices, it's hard to imagine that the first New Englanders considered this delectable seafood humble and ordinary.

Ingredients

4 1-lb live lobsters
Water
Salt or seaweed

1 cup melted butter
Lemon wedges
Parsley sprigs

Fill a large stock pot full of water and add salt or a piece of seaweed. Bring the water to a boil and then turn off the heat. Place the live lobsters in the pot, keeping your hand well away from the claws. Lower them in claws first. Bring the water slowly back to a boil and cook the lobsters for about 15 minutes, or until they turn bright red. Remove them from the water and drain briefly on paper towels. Place on a plate and garnish the plate with lemon wedges and parsley sprigs. Serve with individual dishes of melted butter for dipping.

Maine's fishermen ensure local restaurants have a fresh daily supply of seafood.

Spiced Salmon Steaks

Preparation Time: 15 minutes plus 1 hour standing time
Cooking Time: 12-15 minutes   **Serves:** 4

A blend of spices and sugar makes this easy-to-prepare salmon dish very out of the ordinary.

Ingredients

½ cup soft light brown sugar
1 tbsp ground allspice
1 tbsp dry mustard
1 tbsp grated fresh ginger
4 salmon steaks, 1-inch thick
1 cucumber

1 bunch green onions
2 tbsps butter
1 tbsp lemon juice
2 tsps chopped fresh dill weed
1 tbsp chopped fresh parsley
Salt and pepper

Mix the sugar and spices together and rub the mixture into the surface of both sides of the salmon steaks. Allow the salmon steaks to stand for at least 1 hour in the refrigerator. Meanwhile prepare the vegetables.

Peel the cucumber and cut into quarters lengthwise. Remove the seeds and cut each quarter into 1-inch pieces. Trim the roots from the green onions and trim down some, but not all, of the green part. Put the cucumber and green onions into a saucepan, along with the butter, lemon juice, dill, parsley and seasoning. Cook over a moderate heat for about 10 minutes, or until the cucumber is tender and turning translucent. Put the salmon steaks under a preheated broiler and cook for about 5-6 minutes on each side. Serve with the cucumber and green onion.

Portland Head Lighthouse overlooks the treacherous Maine coast.

Fish Stew

Preparation Time: 20-25 minutes **Cooking Time:** 35 minutes **Serves:** 4

This delicious concoction makes great use of the fresh seafood readily available at New England fish markets.

Ingredients

1 medium onion, finely chopped
2 cloves garlic, crushed
3 tbsps olive oil
1½ lbs tomatoes, skinned, seeded and chopped
2 cups dry red wine
2 tbsps tomato paste

Salt and pepper
4 cups fresh mussels in their shells, scrubbed and debearded
8 large unpeeled shrimp
¾ cup peeled shrimp
4 crab claws, shelled but with claw tips left intact

In a large pan, fry the onion and garlic together gently in the olive oil, until they are soft but not brown. Add the tomatoes and fry until they are beginning to soften. Stir in the red wine and the tomato paste. Season to taste, then bring to a boil. Cover and simmer for about 15 minutes. Add the mussels, re-cover the pan and simmer for 5-8 minutes, or until all the mussel shells are open. Discard any that do not open. Stir in the remaining ingredients and cook, uncovered, for about 5-8 minutes, or until the shellfish is heated through.

Top: a peaceful scene at Stonington, Maine.

Baked Stuffed Mackerel

Preparation Time: 15 minutes **Cooking Time:** 30 minutes **Serves:** 4

This simple but tasty recipe will convert all those who consider mackerel a little too strongly flavored.

Ingredients

¼ cup margarine
1 small onion, finely chopped
⅓ cup fresh whole-wheat
   breadcrumbs
1½ tsps chopped fresh parsley
1 tsp dried thyme

Freshly ground sea salt and
   black pepper
2-3 tbsps hot water if required
4 mackerel, cleaned and
   washed thoroughly

Preheat oven to 375°F. In a large frying pan, melt the margarine. Fry the chopped onion in the margarine until it is soft, but not colored. Add the breadcrumbs, herbs and seasoning to the fried onion, and mix well to form a firm stuffing, adding a little hot water to bind, if necessary. Fill the cavities of the fish with the stuffing and wrap each one separately in well-oiled aluminum foil. Place each fish parcel in a roasting pan, or on a cookie sheet, and cook for half an hour.

Boston's restaurants are famous for their wonderfully fresh seafood specialties.

Seafood Tart

Preparation Time: 40 minutes plus 1 hour refrigeration
Cooking Time: 40 minutes   **Serves:** 6-8

This dish is a wonderful year-round meal because it can be adapted to include whatever seafood is in season.

Ingredients

Pastry
2 cups all-purpose flour, sifted
½ cup unsalted butter
Pinch salt
4 tbsps cold milk

Filling
4 oz sole or cod fillets
8 oz cooked shrimp
4 oz flaked crab meat

½ cup white wine
½ cup water
Large pinch red pepper flakes
Salt and pepper
2 tbsps butter
2 tbsps flour
1 clove garlic, crushed
2 egg yolks
½ cup heavy cream
Chopped fresh parsley

To prepare the pastry, sift the flour into a bowl, cut the butter into small pieces and begin mixing them into the flour. Mix until the mixture resembles fine breadcrumbs. This can also be done in a food processor. Make a well in the flour, pour in the milk and add the salt. Mix with a fork, gradually incorporating the butter and flour mixture until all the ingredients are mixed. Form the dough into a ball and knead for about 1 minute. Leave the dough in the refrigerator for about 1 hour.

To prepare the filling, cook the fish fillets in the wine and water with the red pepper flakes for about 10 minutes or until just firm to the touch. When the fish is cooked, remove it from the liquid and flake it into a bowl with the shrimp and the crab meat. Reserve the cooking liquid. Melt the butter in a small saucepan and stir in the flour. Gradually strain the cooking liquid from the fish, stirring constantly until smooth. Add garlic, place over high heat and bring to a boil. Lower the heat and allow to cook for 1 minute. Add to the fish in the bowl, season and set aside to cool. On a well-floured surface, roll out the pastry and transfer it to a tart pan with a removable base. Press the dough into the pan and cut off any excess. Prick the base lightly with a fork and place a sheet of wax paper inside. Fill with rice, dried beans or baking beans and chill for 30 minutes. Bake the pastry shell for 15 minutes in a 375°F oven. While the pastry is baking, combine the egg yolks, cream and parsley and stir into the fish filling. Adjust the seasoning. Take the pastry shell out of the oven, remove the paper and beans, and pour in the filling. Return the tart to the oven and bake for another 25 minutes. Allow to cool slightly and then remove from the pan. Transfer to a serving dish and slice before serving.

Steamed Fish Rolls

Preparation Time: 25 minutes **Cooking Time:** 10-15 minutes **Serves:** 4

Sole fillets and shrimp make a great combination in this simple dish.

Ingredients

2 large sole, cut into 4 fillets
1 cup peeled shrimp, chopped
2 tsps cornstarch

1 tsp dry sherry
4 green onions, green only, chopped
2 eggs, beaten with a pinch of salt

Skin the fillets carefully and lay them skin side up on a flat surface. Mix the shrimp with the cornstarch, sherry and onions. Divide this mixture equally between the fillets. Cook the eggs in a wok or frying pan, until they are softly scrambled. Spread equal quantities of this over the shrimp mixture. Roll up the fish fillets jelly-roll fashion, folding the thicker end over first. Secure with wooden picks. Put the fish rolls in the top of a steamer or fish kettle and fill the bottom with boiling water. Steam for 10-15 minutes, until the fish is cooked. Remove the wooden picks and serve immediately.

Top: the harbor and Captain's Cove at Bridgeport, Connecticut, where a replica of a British frigate of the Revolutionary War is moored.

Cod Salad

Preparation Time: 2 hours plus 24 hours refrigeration   **Serves:** 4

Raw fish marinated in lime, or seviche, is a delicious combination for which cod is perfect. If you prefer, you can lightly poach the fish in olive oil and vinegar before marinating.

Ingredients

1 lb cod fillets
Juice and grated rind of 2 limes
1 shallot, chopped
1 green chili pepper, seeded and
    finely chopped
1 tsp ground cilantro
1 small green pepper, seeded
    and sliced

1 small red pepper, seeded and sliced
1 tbsp chopped fresh parsley
1 tbsp chopped fresh cilantro leaves
4 green onions, chopped
2 tbsps olive oil
Salt and pepper
1 small head of lettuce

Skin the cod fillets and cut them into thin strips across the grain. Put the cod strips into a bowl, and pour over them the lime juice and rind. Add the shallot, chili pepper and cilantro, and stir well to coat the fish completely. Cover the bowl and refrigerate for 24 hours, stirring occasionally. When ready to serve, drain the fish and stir in the peppers, parsley, cilantro leaves, onions and oil. Season to taste and serve on a bed of lettuce.

New Hampshire's fall colors shade the Union Church at Stark, New Hampshire.

Shrimp Risotto

Preparation Time: 15 minutes **Cooking Time:** 25 minutes **Serves:** 4

New England's waters provide a variety of shrimp – medium-sized shrimp that come about 25 to the pound are best for this recipe.

Ingredients

1 lb unpeeled shrimp	2 tbsps chopped fresh parsley
1 glass white wine	1 cup brown rice
4 fresh tomatoes	1 tsp tomato paste
3 gloves garlic	Freshly ground sea salt and
1 large onion	black pepper
3 tbsps olive oil	2 tbsps grated Parmesan cheese

Peel the shrimp, leaving 4 unpeeled for a garnish. Put the shrimp shells and the wine into a saucepan and bring to a boil. Remove the pan from the heat and allow to cool completely before straining out the shrimp shells. Reserve the liquid. Chop the tomatoes roughly, and remove the cores. Peel and chop the garlic and onion. Heat the olive oil in a large frying pan, or saucepan. Cook the onion and garlic gently in the oil, without browning them. Stir in the parsley and cook for about 30 seconds. Add the rice to the fried onion, and stir well to coat the grains with the oil. Add the wine, tomato paste, tomatoes and just enough cold water to cover the rice. Season the rice with salt and pepper, and cook for about 20 minutes, until all the water is absorbed and the rice is tender. When the rice is cooked, stir in the peeled shrimp and the cheese. Heat through gently, place in a serving dish and top with the unpeeled shrimp.

The Pemaquid Peninsula in Maine is dotted with quiet, picturesque coves.

Seafood Stew

Preparation Time: 35 minutes **Cooking Time:** 20 minutes **Serves:** 6

Clams are crucial to this stew so buy the freshest you can find – littlenecks and cherrystones are favorites in New England.

Ingredients

24 clams in the shell
3 squid, cleaned and cut into rings
2 lbs firm whitefish, filleted into
   2-inch pieces
3 medium-sized tomatoes, peeled,
   seeded and chopped
½ green pepper, seeded
   and chopped

1 small onion, chopped
1 clove garlic, finely chopped
1 cup dry white wine
Salt and pepper
½ cup olive oil
6 slices French bread
3 tbsps chopped parsley

Scrub the clams well to remove any barnacles. Discard any with broken shells or ones that do not close when tapped. Place the clams in a large saucepan or heatproof casserole, scatter over them about half of the vegetables and garlic and spoon over 4 tbsps of the olive oil.

Scatter the squid and the prepared whitefish over the vegetables in the pan and top with the remaining vegetables. Pour in the white wine and season with salt and pepper. Bring to a boil over high heat and then reduce to simmering. Cover the pan and cook for about 20 minutes or until the clams open, the squid is tender and the fish flakes easily. Discard any clams that do not open. Heat the remaining olive oil in a frying pan and when hot, add the slices of bread, browning them well on both sides. Drain on paper towels. Place a slice of bread in the bottom of a soup bowl and ladle the fish mixture over the bread. Sprinkle with parsley and serve immediately.

Cod Curry

Preparation Time: 15 minutes **Cooking Time:** about 20 minutes **Serves:** 4

Cod is plentiful in Cape waters from March right through to September, so try this recipe when you get tired of more ordinary cod dishes.

Ingredients

3 tbsps vegetable oil
1 large onion, peeled and chopped
1-inch piece cinnamon stick
1 bay leaf
1 tsp ginger powder
1 tsp garlic powder
1 tsp chili powder
1 tsp ground cumin
1 tsp ground cilantro
¼ tsp ground turmeric

½ cup natural yogurt or
  8-oz can tomatoes, chopped
1-2 fresh green chilies, chopped
2 sprigs fresh cilantro leaves,
  chopped
1 tsp salt
1lb cod cutlets, or fillets, cut into
  2-inch pieces

In a large heavy-based saucepan, fry the onion in the oil until golden brown. Add the cinnamon, bay leaf, ginger and garlic and fry for 1 minute. Add the ground spices and fry for a further minute, then stir in either the yogurt, or the canned tomatoes and the chopped chilies and cilantro leaves.

Only if you have used yogurt, stir in ½ cup water and simmer the mixture for 2-3 minutes. Do not add any water if you have used the canned tomatoes. Stir the cod into the sauce, and add the salt. Cover the pan and simmer for 15-18 minutes before serving.

Mystic Seaport, founded in 1929, recreates a New England seaport of old.

Fish Escabech

Preparation Time: about 25 minutes, with 24 hours refrigeration
Cooking Time: about 25 minutes   **Serves:** 6

Monkfish is a good choice for this recipe as it has a good firm texture.
Originally, this method of marinating sautéed fish in vinegar was simply a way
of preserving it.

Ingredients

3 lbs monkfish
6 tbsps flour
Pinch salt and pepper
1 medium carrot, peeled and
   thinly sliced
1 medium onion, thinly sliced

1 bay leaf
2 sprigs parsley
¼-½ fresh red chili, finely chopped
1½ cups white wine vinegar
6 cloves garlic, peeled and thinly sliced
Olive oil

Peel the brownish membrane from the outside of the monkfish tails. Cut along
the bone with a sharp filleting knife to separate the flesh from it. Cut the
monkfish into slices about 1-inch thick. Mix the salt and pepper with the flour
and dredge the slices of monkfish, shaking off the excess flour. Fry in olive oil
until golden brown. Remove and drain on paper towels. Add the carrot and
onion and fry gently for about 5 minutes. Add the bay leaf, parsley, vinegar,
chili pepper and 1 cup water. Cover and simmer gently for about 20 minutes.
Place the fish in a shallow casserole dish and pour over the marinade.
Sprinkle on the sliced garlic and cover well. Refrigerate for 24 hours, turning
the fish over several times.
    To serve, remove the fish from the marinade and arrange on a serving
plate. Pour the marinade on top of the fish and garnish with parsley, if desired.

Fishing and tourism are the mainstays of Provincetown's economy.

Appetizers:
Cape Cod Mussels 22
Mussels in Red Wine 30
Oysters à la Crème 20
Salmon Pâté 18
Scallops in Saffron
    Sauce 24
Baked Stuffed Mackerel 56
Boatman's Stew 48
Boiled Maine Lobster 50
Boston Scrod 44
Cape Cod Mussels 22
Clam Chowder 12
Cod Curry 68
Cod Salad 62
Eel in Red Wine 36
Fish Escabech 70
Fish Stew 54
Fried Squid 28
Lobster Salad 42
Main Course Dishes:
Baked Stuffed Mackerel 56
Boatman's Stew 48
Boiled Maine Lobster 50
Boston Scrod 44
Cod Curry 68
Eel in Red Wine 36
Fish Escabech 70
Fish Stew 54
Fried Squid 28
Monkfish Kebabs with Butter
    Sauce 32
Salt Cod with Peppers 38
Seafood Stew 66
Seafood Tart 58

Shrimp Risotto 64
Spiced Salmon Steaks 52
Steamed Fish Rolls 60
Swordfish Kebabs 26
Swordfish Steaks with Peppercorn
    and Garlic Sauce 40
Whole Baked Fish with New
    England Stuffing 46
Monkfish Kebabs with Butter Sauce 32
Mussel Soup 14
Mussels in Red Wine 30
New England Bouillabaise 16
Oysters à la Crème 20
Salads:
Cod Salad 62
Lobster Salad 42
Shrimp Salad 34
Salmon Paté 18
Salt Cod with Peppers 38
Scallops in Saffron Sauce 24
Seafood Stew 66
Seafood Tart 58
Shrimp Risotto 64
Shrimp Salad 34
Soups:
Clam Chowder 12
Mussel Soup 14
New England Bouillabaisse 16
Spiced Salmon Steaks 52
Steamed Fish Rolls 60
Swordfish Kebabs 26
Swordfish Steaks with Peppercorn and
    Garlic Sauce 40
Whole Baked Fish with New England
    Stuffing 46